Vintage-Style
Beaded Jewelry

Vintage-Style
Beaded
Jewelry

35 BEAUTIFUL PROJECTS
USING NEW AND OLD MATERIALS

Deborah Schneebeli-Morrell

CICO BOOKS
LONDON NEW YORK

DEDICATION
To Lily Rendong Laurie, a beautiful girl who so loved modeling all the jewelry in this book.

ACKNOWLEDGMENTS
I would like to thank my friends Anthea Sieveking, Annie Rothenstein, Nan Farquharson, Jill Newsome, and my mother Dalia Beilin Morrell for their kindness and for inspiring me with beads, jewelry, and props. As ever, I am really grateful to Gloria Nicol for all her specialist help and encouragement, and for taking the lovely photographs in the book. A big thank you to Cindy Richards for the commission and to Georgina Harris for her friendly and humorous chivvying. Lastly, many thanks to Gillian Haslam for the clear, simple, and as always, trouble-free editing. Thank you also to Angel At My Table for the loan of lovely props.

First published in 2004 by CICO Books
This edition published in 2011 by CICO Books
an imprint of Ryland Peters and Small
519 Broadway, 5th Floor, New York, NY 10012
20–21 Jockey's Fields, London, WC1R 4BW
www.cicobooks.com

10 9 8 7 6 5 4 3 2 1

A CIP catalogue record for this book is available from the Library of Congress and the British Library.

ISBN: 978-1-907563-10-2

Printed in China

Edited by Gillian Haslam
Photography by Gloria Nicol
Designed by David Fordham
Illustrated by Kate Simunek

Contents

Tools and Techniques

TOOLS AND EQUIPMENT

Y OU NEED VERY FEW SPECIAL TOOLS to begin beading. A beading mat is useful to stop the beads rolling around too much, and tweezers can be useful for picking up tiny seed beads. Most importantly, you will need a pair of small jeweler's pliers as well as soft wirecutters. Epoxy glue is the best adhesive to use as it sticks permanently to surfaces such as glass, metal, and china, although white craft glue is best for sticking fabric.

BEADS

T HE ASIAN SUBCONTINENT AND EUROPE (particularly Venice, where the incredible art of beaded flower-making originated) are great sources of beautiful glass beads. Specialist bead shops are the most wonderful places and usually have thousands of different sorts of beads in stock. It is a good idea to buy an assorted bead pack when you start. These contain beads in many shapes, sizes, and colors, and provide an inexpensive alternative to buying individual beads. There are also many mail order catalogs and websites.

A NTIQUE AND FLEA MARKETS are other wonderful sources, where there are often stalls specializing in jewelry and you can buy vintage pieces that can be easily dismantled to re-assemble in your own design. Markets are also a good source for assorted charms, costume jewelry, and stunning but inexpensive diamanté. Junk shops, thrift stores, and charity shops provide other useful hunting grounds. Family hand-me-downs or heirlooms can also be re-used, such as an old pearl necklace that may need re-stringing or a collection of turquoise nuggets. Many people have a button box containing old buttons just perfect for jewelry. If not, lovely buttons are available from trimmings or haberdashery shops. The tiny seed beads are also known as rocailles. Bugle beads are shaped like tubes.

Other materials

Wire

Beads can be threaded onto different types of material depending on the type and style of piece. Tiger tail is a stainless steel wire coated in nylon that comes in a number of colors and in two thicknesses. It is strong and flexible, easy to thread, and won't tangle or kink. It is ideal for threading a necklace.

Bonded nylon thread can be also used. This is ideal when making a more complicated beading pattern such as the daisy chain for spectacles on page 19. It is available in black, white, and many colors.

Daisy chain

Beaded flower corsage

Fine jewelry wire is more pliable. It can be twisted and bent to accommodate intricate beading techniques, such as the beaded flower corsage on page 34 or the filigree choker on page 100. It is available in silver or silver- or gold-plated as well as in brass, copper, and a number of anodized aluminum colors. It comes in a range of thicknesses from ¹⁄₆₄in. (0.4mm) to ⅜in. (1.5mm). The thickness is also referred to as the "gauge" of the wire.

Memory wire—a standard length coil which retains its shape—can be finished with a loop in the wire (as on page 110), or by fitting and gluing a stop bead.

Elastic

Elastic is used when making bracelets instead of using a clasp. The ½in. (0.5mm) version can be knotted, but the thicker version needs to be joined neatly with a crimp bead. It is available in several colors.

Chain

Available as solid silver or silver- or gold-plated, link designs can be bought by length or weight. Chain is used for the charm bracelet on page 14. It may be necessary to cut it with heavier (rather than wirecutters) depending on its thickness.

Charm bracelet

FINDINGS

*T*HIS IS THE TERM USED TO DESCRIBE the clasps, earring loops and fish hooks, and jumprings used in the jewelry projects.

*C*LASPS COME IN MANY STYLES AND SIZES, so select the appropriate one to complement your design. You can choose between barrel clasp, the common spring ring, lobster claw, or hook and eye. Many of these are available in solid silver or gold plate at a reasonable cost. Also consider using old clasps which have been saved from dismantled or junk jewelry.

*B*ROOCH PINS CAN BE USED, as with the blue-and-white cameo brooches on page 75. Attach them to the back of your creation with epoxy glue.

Blue-and-white cameo brooch

*H*EAD PINS OR EYE PINS ARE USED to attach beads to a chain (see the charm bracelet on page 14).

*R*OUND OR CLAM SHELL CALOTTES are covers for a knot or crimp bead end on a strung necklace. They close over the knot or bead and the hook is connected to the necklace clasp.

Charm bracelet

BASIC TECHNIQUES

*T*HERE ARE VERY FEW SPECIAL TECHNIQUES used in the projects in this book, but here are a few useful tips for fitting clasps, spacing beads, and attaching head pins.

Threading beads on nylon thread

*W*HEN THREADING BEADS onto a length of nylon thread, it is useful to tie the end of the thread around a larger bead to act as a temporary stop.

Fitting jump rings

When using jump rings, be sure to close the rings securely, using the tips of your pliers.

Fitting clam shells

When using clam shell clasps, bring the strand(s) of wire through the clasp and then through a crimp bead. Crush the crimp bead with pliers and cut off any excess wire, then close the clam shell.

Fitting multi-wires to a clasp

Bring the strands of wire through a crimp bead, then through the small ring on the clasp. Bend the strands back through the crimp bead. Pull tightly, squash the crimp bead with pliers, and cut off any excess wire.

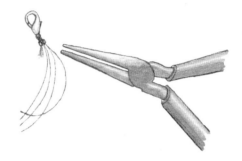

Fitting barrel clasps

When using barrel clasps, bring the wire up through a crimp bead, through the ring on one end of the barrel clasp, and back through the crimp bead. Crush the crimp bead with pliers, then cut off any excess wire.

Spacing beads

To space beads on a wire, thread a crimp bead on either side of the main bead, and crush with pliers to hold the main bead in place.

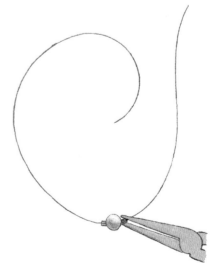

Threading beads onto a head pin

Thread the required beads onto the head pin and connect the pin to the chain by bending over and into a link. Cut off excess wire and close the loop to secure.

Joining elastic

When joining elastic, use a crimp bead rather than a knot which can look unsightly. Thread both ends of the elastic through either side of the crimp bead. Crush it with pliers to secure in place, then cut off any excess elastic.

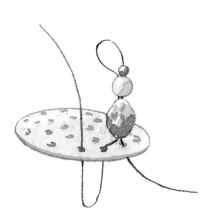

Using an earring sieve

Using a length of wire, weave the beads onto the sieve by taking the wire up through one hole, threading on the beads, then taking the wire down through an adjacent hole. Pull the wire tightly to anchor the beads in place.

Treasured Gifts

*I*T IS HARD TO IMAGINE a more welcome gift than a lovingly made piece of jewelry. While for many of us it is so easy to go out and buy something that is mass-produced, the recipient of your gift will feel so much more special when you present a unique piece made especially for them. You will find that not only can you create an original piece of jewelry, but make it for a fraction of the cost of a store-bought piece. Perhaps you know someone who would really love and use the spectacle daisy chain, while the beaded flower earrings would suit a younger person. The beaded flower corsage is a spectacular gift to someone of any age who will appreciate the inspiration and skill involved in its making. Using the simplest techniques, there are projects in this chapter to suit all tastes, and in their making you will develop the skills to move onto slightly more involved projects.

Mirrored Charm Bracelet

MIRROR-EFFECT GLASS BEADS are the perfect partners for these surprisingly inexpensive silver hearts, while pretty glass beads shimmer with deep pastel, light-reflecting foil centers. This delicate charm bracelet would make a wonderful present for a treasured friend on a special occasion. You could also make a child's version, replacing the real silver charms with brightly colored beads.

Materials

18in. (45cm) real silver chain, in cable design
½in. (13mm) hook and eye clasp
2 ⅜in. (9.5mm) silver jump rings
Silver head pins
Silver eye pins
Foil-lined glass beads in assorted shapes

3 silver hearts
9 silver spacer beads in different shapes
Faceted roundel glass beads
Pliers
Wirecutters

How to make a Mirrored Charm Bracelet

1 (Above) Cut the chain to a length to fit loosely around your wrist. At one end add the eye to the chain using a jump ring. Close the jump ring with the pliers.

2 (Above) At the other end of the chain, add the hook in the same manner, using the second jump ring and closing the ring with the pliers.

3 (Above right) Decide how closely you want to space the charms and beads—on this bracelet, for example, they are added to every fifth link. Thread an eye pin through a round bead, open the eye slightly at the bottom, and push the open end through a silver heart. Press together with pliers to close.

4 (Above) Place the head pin through the second chain ring, bend over with the pliers. Cut off the excess and turn over to make a secure ring.

6 (Right) Continue adding assorted glass beads, and silver hearts, either using eye pins or head pins, and attaching them to every fifth link. The last charm can be attached to one side of the eye so, when the clasp is closed, the bracelet is evenly spaced.

5 (Right) Fit a small bead with a head pin. Thread the head pin with a larger bead, as shown, and place the top end through a link of chain. Bend over, cut, and secure into a ring.

Silver Chain Jeweled Necklace

ALTERNATIVE

*T*his extravagant silver chain necklace is made in a similar way to the previous project, using a real silver lobster clasp and silver head pins or eye pins. A wonderful assortment of pressed glass beads, faceted fire-polished glass, shimmering crystals, diamanté rondels, and classic imitation teardrop pearls in all sizes are suspended from the chain, creating a truly theatrical necklace rich in color and texture, and overloaded with light-catching jewels. There are even two small chandelier crystals to draw attention.

Spectacle Daisy Chain

*T*HIS PRETTY DESIGN is very satisfying to make, with its repeat pattern and two-tone color scheme. Use a nylon thread of sufficient strength to support the glasses. Choose beads in colors to match a favorite outfit or the color of the frames. You could also use the same technique to make a child's bracelet, simply substituting elastic thread for the nylon.

Materials

Thick bonded nylon
   thread (or thin, if
   your chosen beads
   have a narrow hole)
450 ¹⁄₁₆in. (2mm) white
   seed beads
90 ⅛in. (3mm) black
   seed beads
2 small silver crimp
   beads
Attachment ends for
   glasses
Beading needle
Pliers

How to make a Spectacle Daisy Chain

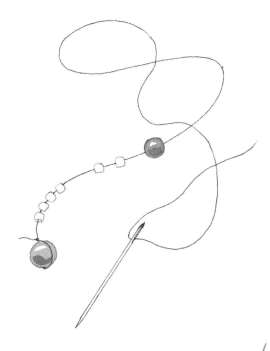

2 (Above) Create half a daisy by re-threading the nylon back through the first white bead.

1 (Above) Cut a 60in. (1.5m) length of nylon thread and thread onto a needle. Tie one end of the thread around a larger bead to act as a temporary stop. Thread on six white beads, followed by one black bead.

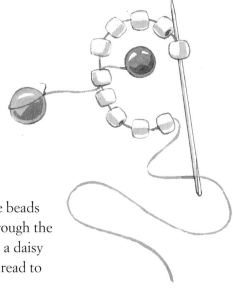

3 (Right) Add four more white beads and thread the needle back through the sixth white bead, thus creating a daisy with a black center. Pull the thread to tighten the flower.

4 (Left) Add a black bead to act as a spacer between the daisies. Pull the nylon tight. Repeat this threading sequence until you have a string of approximately 45 daisies. Remember to pull the nylon thread tightly all the time so none of the thread shows between the daisies.

5 (Right) Thread a small crimp bead onto the nylon before you add the last black bead. Thread the nylon through the ring onto the spectacle attachment loop, then back through the black bead and the crimp bead. Pull the thread to tighten, then crush the crimp bead between the pliers. Remove the temporary stop bead from the other end, and secure and attach the second loop in exactly the same manner.

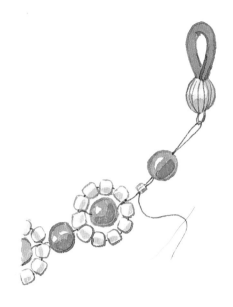

Teardrop Ankle Bracelet

*T*HIS IS ONE OF THE SIMPLEST PROJECTS in the book and it does make a great gift for a young girl. You might like to try using real silver for the chain and good beads for the best effect, and aim to keep the design relatively simple. Here a plain, real silver toggle clasp has been used, which is easy to open and close, with pretty lilac clear glass teardrop beads threaded onto real silver head pins attached to a length of silver chain. You can easily adjust the size of the chain to fit the individual ankle. You could also create a necklace and wrist bracelet, to make a set.

Materials

Silver cable chain, 8½in.
  (22cm) long or to
  fit ankle
Solid silver toggle clasp
2 silver jump rings
12 pressed glass lilac
  teardrop beads
12 silver head pins
Wirecutters
Pliers

How to make an Ankle Bracelet

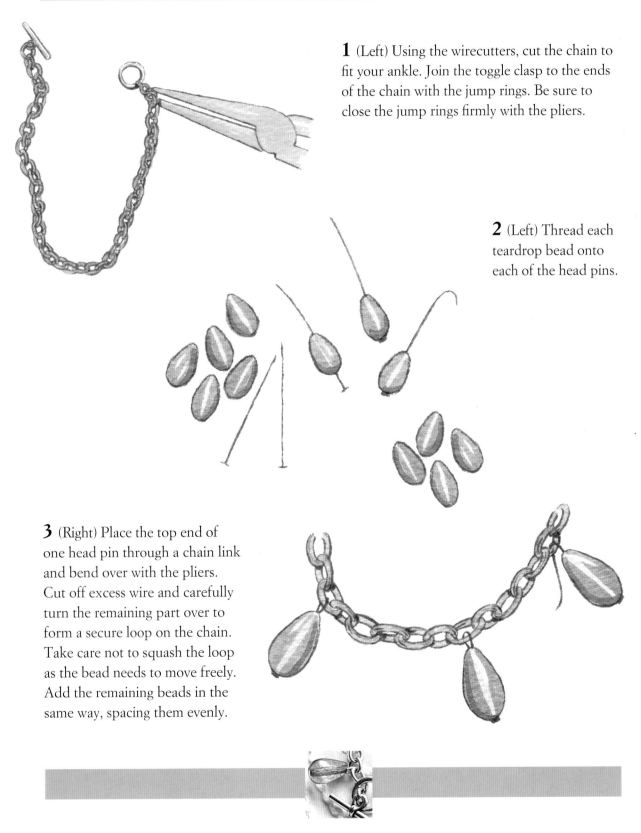

1 (Left) Using the wirecutters, cut the chain to fit your ankle. Join the toggle clasp to the ends of the chain with the jump rings. Be sure to close the jump rings firmly with the pliers.

2 (Left) Thread each teardrop bead onto each of the head pins.

3 (Right) Place the top end of one head pin through a chain link and bend over with the pliers. Cut off excess wire and carefully turn the remaining part over to form a secure loop on the chain. Take care not to squash the loop as the bead needs to move freely. Add the remaining beads in the same way, spacing them evenly.

Diamanté Flowered Earrings

*T*HESE BRILLIANT AND GLITTERING, COLORFUL DIAMANTE FLOWERS were found in a fleamarket. Luckily they have a loop at both the top and the base which makes them adaptable and easy to work with. Although inexpensive, they add a dazzling touch of opulence to these pretty drop crystal earrings. Pale pink, blue, and yellow bicone crystals formed into a loop are suspended from gold fish hooks, catching the light. This jewelry would look wonderful with eveningwear—just the thing to set off a little black dress.

Materials

Tiger tail (nylon-coated stainless steel wire)

13 ⅛in. (3mm) bicone pink crystals

13 ⅛in. (3mm) bicone yellow crystals

13 ⅛in. (3mm) bicone blue crystals

6 multicolored diamanté flowers

10 small gold crimp beads

2 gold fish hook earrings

2 pink faceted glass beads

Wirecutters

Pliers

How to make Diamanté Flowered Earrings

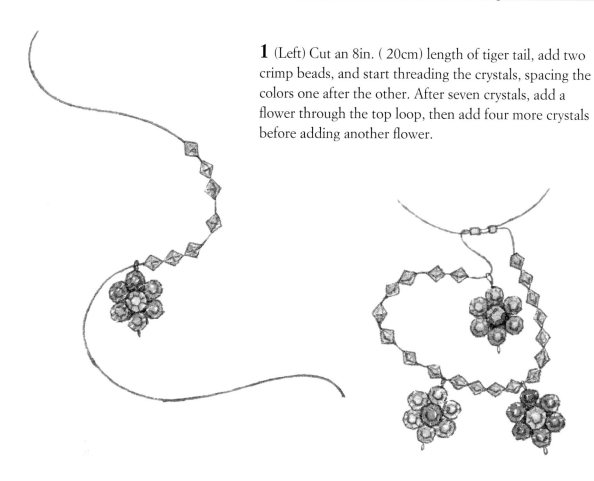

1 (Left) Cut an 8in. (20cm) length of tiger tail, add two crimp beads, and start threading the crystals, spacing the colors one after the other. After seven crystals, add a flower through the top loop, then add four more crystals before adding another flower.

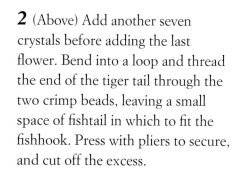

2 (Above) Add another seven crystals before adding the last flower. Bend into a loop and thread the end of the tiger tail through the two crimp beads, leaving a small space of fishtail in which to fit the fishhook. Press with pliers to secure, and cut off the excess.

3 (Left) Cut three 2in. (5cm) lengths of tiger tail. Thread each one through the base loop of the flowers, bend over in the center, and take the two ends back through a crystal and a crimp bead. Pull tightly, crush the crimp bead, and cut off the excess. Use one of each color of the crystals on each flower.

4 (Right) Attach the fish hook between a crimp bead on the top of the crystal loop.

If you would like to thread a glass bead onto the shaft of the fish hook, first open up the loop at the base. Take off the gold bead that comes with the hook, thread on the glass bead, replace the gold one, and secure the hook back around the loop of the earring.

Flower and Sequin Earrings

*T*HESE DELICATE EARRINGS use tiny, straight-sided beads in a range of metallic colors. The beading technique is called French beading, but the craft actually originated in Venice and was used in religious art, to make altarpieces and funeral wreaths. This skill experienced a revival of interest in Victorian times and again in the 1930s and 40s. Once you have mastered the technique, you can patiently build up a bouquet of pretty beaded flowers.

Materials

½in. (0.5mm) pink thin-walled glass seed beads

28 gauge copper beading wire

2 domed ear clips with sieves, ⅝in. (1.5cm) in diameter

12 pink iridescent faceted sequins

12 ⅟₁₆in. (2mm) orange seed beads

Wirecutters

How to make Flower and Sequin Earrings

1 (Left) Cut a length of wire approximately 36in. (90cm) long for each petal (you'll need five in total). Bend the wire 5in. (12.5cm) from one end and twist, making a 2½in. (6cm) loop. Thread nine pink beads onto the remaining short end of the wire. Thread approximately ten pink beads onto the longer length.

2 (Right) Twist the beaded wire around the shorter central wire. Thread another ten pink beads onto the wire, bend it down and twist around the base of the central stem.

3 (Above) Thread more beads onto the wire, increasing the number of beads on each side to accommodate the increase in size of the petal. Add one bead onto the central stem at the top before twisting the longer wire around.

4 (Left) Continue in this way, adding one more bead onto the top central wire when you twist the wire around. Bind the wire tightly and neatly around the loop at the base of the petal to secure. Add another bead to the top central wire, twist the wire over the bead twice, and cut on the reverse side. Repeat this process until you have five petals, then thread the wire stems of each petal through the holes around the outside of the sieve.

5 (Below) Cut a 12in. (30cm) length of wire and thread through from the back between the petals, through a sequin and a small orange bead, and through another hole in the sieve. Pull tightly and bring through to the front, sewing on sequins and beads so there are five around the edge of the petals and one in the center. Bring the wire to the back, twist to secure.

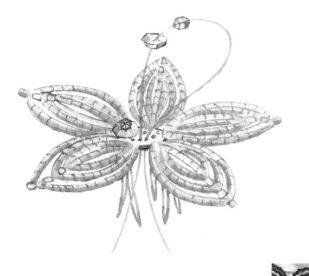

6 Turn the flower over and twist all the petal stems tightly. Cut off excess ends and press down into the well of the sieve. Place the domed ear clip onto the sieve and bend over the clips to secure the flower. Make a matching earring in the same way.

Beaded Flower Corsage

*T*HIS IS A LOVELY VARIATION of the French beading technique used for the earrings on the previous pages. The small white beads are very restrained in effect, emphasizing the shape and the technique. The stamens on the flowers are simply lengths of wire threaded with identical white seed beads and then folded in half. Add four or five stamens and bind all the ends together with the petals. The corsage is made by wiring the three flowers into a spray, then binding the whole piece tightly with white cotton embroidery thread, securing the ends with a dab of white craft glue. It would look good decorating a lapel or the brim of a hat.

Three-Strand Metallic Necklace

*T*HIS SIMPLE YET STUNNING STRANDED NECKLACE would look fantastic worn with the memory wire bracelet featured on page 110. This necklace is a great design for using up assorted beads left over from other jewelry projects. Each strand features a different repeated pattern and has a vintage appearance in warm shades of gold, bronze, and pink.

Materials

STRAND 1
⅛in. (3mm) pink metallic bugle beads
Dark fire-polished glass beads

STRAND 2
⅛in. (3mm) pink metallic bugle beads
¼in. (6mm) iridescent green twisted glass bugle beads
Dull, pale green fire-polished faceted glass beads

STRAND 3
⅛in. (3mm) pink metallic bugle beads
⅛in. (3mm) fat bronze glass bugle beads
Small round purple glass beads
¼in. (6mm) clear iridescent faceted beads

2 silver clam shell knot covers
2 large silver crimp beads
Barrel clasp
Pink tiger tail (nylon-coated stainless steel wire)
Pliers
Wirecutters

How to make a Three-Strand Metallic Necklace

1 (Left) Make the first strand. Thread on 17 pink bugle beads, followed by one dark glass bead. Follow this with 14 pink bugles, then a dark bead. Repeat until eight dark beads are in place, then finish off with 17 pink bugles. Place to one side, making sure that the beads do not fall off at either end.

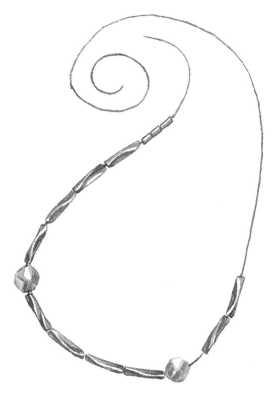

2 (Right) To make the second strand, thread three small pink bugles, followed by four long twisted bugles. Add a green faceted bead, then repeat this pattern until all eight green beads are in place. Finish with four long bugles, followed by three tiny pink ones. Set aside.

3 (Right) To make the third strand, thread two small pink bugles, followed by eight bronze glass bugles, followed by a round purple bead, a clear iridescent faceted bead, another round purple bead, and eight bronze bugles. Continue in this way until there are ten bead interruptions along the bugle length. Remember to match the other end with two small pink bugles.

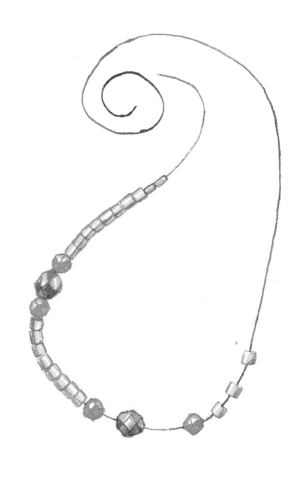

4 (Above) Bring the three ends of the strands together. Thread through a clam shell and then through a crimp bead. Crush the crimp bead, cut off any excess wire, and close the clam shell. Repeat on the other end.

5 (Above) Using pliers, bend the hook end of the clam shell around the ring on each end of the barrel clasp.

The use of the different beads will result in the three strands varying slightly in length, adding to the design.

Floral Hair Band

THIS SUBTLE, ANTIQUE GREEN, SOFT VELVET RIBBON makes the ideal background on which to embroider a pretty floral design. The little pressed velvet flowers, so evocative of an earlier time where they would have been used to decorate felt hats, are available at a good haberdashery or notions stores or specialist ribbon stores. Sequins and small beads are often used in combination to embroider textiles, particularly in the Indian subcontinent. Once you have experimented with the hair band, you may like to extend your skills and embroider a cardigan or a special evening dress. Match your beads and sequins carefully against a darker background and the result will be quite exotic. The hair band could also easily be adapted as a choker—just measure the ribbon around your own neck, allowing for turning the ends and adding the tie.

Materials

20in. (50cm) green velvet
   ribbon, 1in. (2.5cm)
   wide
5 burnt orange pressed
   velvet flowers, ⅝in.
   (1.5cm) in diameter
12 turquoise sequin leaves
5 round sequins
⅛in. (3mm) turquoise
   glass bugle beads
5 ⅛in. (3mm) cut glass
   turquoise beads
Needle and invisible
   thread
16in. (40cm) green rayon
   or silk ribbon, ½in.
   (13mm) wide

How to make a Floral Hair Band

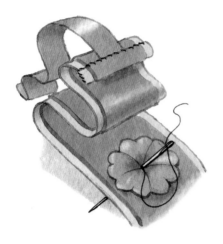

2 (Right) Sew a circular turquoise sequin onto the center of each flower and top with a cut-glass bead. Fasten the thread neatly on the back of the ribbon behind each flower.

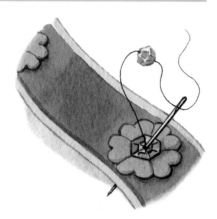

1 (Above) Cut the velvet ribbon to fit around your head with a 1in. (2.5cm) gap between the ends. Cut the silk ribbon in half. Turn over the cut ends of the velvet ribbon, insert one of the silk ribbon ends into the fold, and stitch in place. Turn over and stitch the other ends of the silk ribbon to prevent fraying. Sew on the flowers 2—3in. (5—7.5cm) apart along the center of the ribbon.

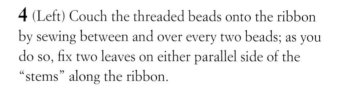

3 (Above right) Starting 2in. (5cm) from one end, bring the thread through to the front of the ribbon, adding bugle beads onto the thread to reach just under the petals of the flower. Continue until you finish the row, working behind each flower.

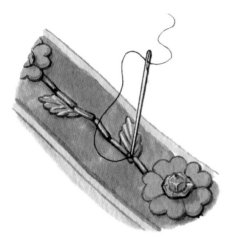

4 (Left) Couch the threaded beads onto the ribbon by sewing between and over every two beads; as you do so, fix two leaves on either parallel side of the "stems" along the ribbon.

Retro Revival

*T*HIS INSPIRING CHAPTER makes reference to materials and fashions from the past. Who hasn't marveled at the variety and subtle iridescent quality of old pearl buttons or sorted through a grandmother's collection of colored buttons and wondered how to use them in a new way—the button necklaces will show you how. Maybe you have an old jewelry box with odd jewels, dusty unwashed beads and pearls, or a bold and beautiful paste pendant that can be reassembled into a stunning necklace. The 1940s pendant necklace has been made from clear flower brooches, very fashionable in the 40s and still widely available from thrift stores and flea markets. Indeed, flea markets, antiques fairs, and garage sales are all wonderful sources of original material that can be redesigned and given a new lease of life. The blue-and-white cameo brooches are a delight and, with the bronze and cut-glass beads framing them, look quite authentic.

Button Necklace

*T*HERE IS SUCH A WONDERFUL ARRAY OF BUTTONS available, both old and new, that you can have enormous fun mixing and matching colors, shapes, and styles. Many people have inherited a button box from a mother or grandmother, full of these treasures and dating from a time when everyone sewed. This unusual project provides the perfect use for these buttons. The beauty of the necklace is that it is completely reversible because two rows of buttons are used to hide the wire that joins them together. This also makes it far more substantial. It is an incredibly simple piece of jewelry to make—the only skill required is in choosing the colors.

Materials

40 buttons in bright colors, such as blue, green, pink, orange, lime green, and yellow

Green or gold tiger tail (nylon-coated stainless steel wire)

2 small gold crimp beads

Gold barrel clasp

Pliers

Wirecutters

How to make a Button Necklace

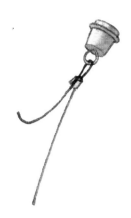

2 (Left) Thread the tiger tail from underneath the first button, back through the second hole and into the first hole of the second button. Bring it up through the second hole and pull firmly, thus securing the second button halfway under the first.

1 (Above) Cut a 25in. (65cm) length of tiger tail. Thread one of the crimp beads onto one end. Pass this end through the ring on one side of the barrel clasp, then back through the crimp bead. Squash the bead with the pliers to secure.

3 (Above) Continue in this manner, bringing the tiger tail up through the top button and down through the lower one. This has the effect of making a staggered double row.

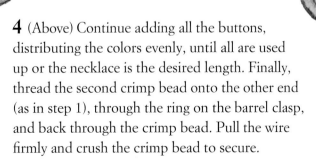

4 (Above) Continue adding all the buttons, distributing the colors evenly, until all are used up or the necklace is the desired length. Finally, thread the second crimp bead onto the other end (as in step 1), through the ring on the barrel clasp, and back through the crimp bead. Pull the wire firmly and crush the crimp bead to secure.

Pearl Button Necklace

ALTERNATIVE

*T*HIS MORE ELABORATE VERSION of the button necklace on the preceding pages is just perfect for eveningwear. This sophisticated variation glints and sparkles in the light and the additional threading of the small faceted glass beads, along with the pretty marquasite and diamanté buttons in the center, gives it a special precious and elegant touch. If you can find them, try to use some older or antique pearl buttons and mix them with contemporary ones. Pearl buttons are actually made from the tropical abalone shell which shimmers with iridescence. Using tiger tail makes the necklace more flexible, whereas using beading wire keeps the buttons more firmly in place.

1940s-style Pendant Necklace

Y OU CAN BUY THESE LOVELY CLEAR PLASTIC BROOCHES in antique shops and flea markets. The flower picture is etched from behind and the indentations are colored to form the image on the front. In this project, the faded colors are complemented by beads rescued from old necklaces. You can use plastic as well as glass beads—plastic beads were also very popular in the 1940s and 50s. Twist the tiger tail attached to the brooches so that it sits well below the beads.

Materials

3 1940s flower brooches

Pink tiger tail (nylon-coated stainless steel wire)

10 small 2in. (5cm) frosted green glass beads

12 small 2in. (5cm) frosted pink glass beads

8 large faceted pink plastic beads

4 medium faceted pink plastic beads

4 small faceted pink plastic beads

2 clam shell knot covers

½in. (13mm) spring ring and jump ring

2 silver crimp beads

Epoxy glue

Wirecutters

Pliers

How to make a 1940s-style Pendant Necklace

1 (Left and right) Cut three 1¼in. (3cm) lengths of wire. Bend in half and place on the back of each brooch to form a hanging loop. Mix the epoxy glue according to the packet instructions. Hold the folded wires in place, then dab the mixed glue over the ends of the wire, and hold in place for 5 minutes, until set.

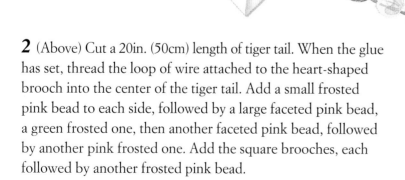

2 (Above) Cut a 20in. (50cm) length of tiger tail. When the glue has set, thread the loop of wire attached to the heart-shaped brooch into the center of the tiger tail. Add a small frosted pink bead to each side, followed by a large faceted pink bead, a green frosted one, then another faceted pink bead, followed by another pink frosted one. Add the square brooches, each followed by another frosted pink bead.

3 (Left) Thread half the remaining beads onto the other side of the necklace as shown, making sure you alternate the sizes and colors of beads to give a pleasing appearance.

4 (Above) Thread a clam shell onto the tiger tail so that it touches the last bead. Push a silver crimp bead onto the wire to nestle in the open clam shell. Crush it onto the wire with the pliers so the tiger tail is secure. Cut off the excess wire.

Close the clam shell over the crimped end of the wire. Loop the hook of the clam shell over the jump ring.

Thread the corresponding beads onto the other end of the necklace, matching the order of the beads, and close the necklace in the same way, using the spring ring.

Glistening Turquoise Bracelet

*T*HIS TWO-STRAND BRACELET RECYCLES METAL-BACKED JEWELS rescued from a broken item of jewelry, making an inexpensive way to create something new. This pretty bracelet would be ideal for a young girl, and even a child can make it as it uses elastic rather than wire for threading. Measure your wrist before you cut the elastic and adjust the length specified in step 1 if necessary.

Materials

Green beading elastic

⅛in. (3mm) clear turquoise glass seed beads

Shield-shaped metal-backed jewels, with 2 channels in the back—4 emerald green, 4 pale blue, and 4 pink

2 silver crimp beads

Pliers

Scissors

How to make a Glistening Turquoise Bracelet

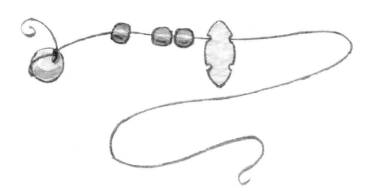

1 (Left) Cut two lengths of elastic, each approximately 12in. (30cm) long. As a temporary ending, tie one end around a bead (this is to stop the beads falling off). Thread one length of the elastic with three turquoise glass beads, then thread the elastic through one channel on the back of a pink jewel.

2 (Right) Add three more glass beads, followed by a green jewel, then three more glass beads, followed by a blue jewel.

3 (Left) When all 12 jewels are threaded onto the elastic, undo the end tied around the extra bead. Thread both ends through the same crimp bead from either side, pulling the elastic firmly so the beads all sit together. Crush the crimp together with pliers.

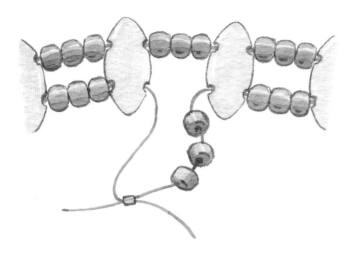

4 (Left) Thread an identical number of turquoise beads to form the second strand, then thread the elastic through the second channel on the back of the jewels. Finish off the bracelet with a crimp bead as in step 3.

Elasticated Sequin and Bead Bracelets

ALTERNATIVE

CREATED USING ASSORTED LEFTOVER BEADS AND SEQUINS, a number of these pretty brightly colored bracelets can be worn together, like Indian bangles. Assortment packs of different shaped and colored sequins are ideal for this project as they contain faceted, star, and flower shapes. Also, try threading a number of sequins together as well as using them separately, and add the odd special bead. Clear beading elastic is used and the beads are fixed in place with a crimp bead.

Pearl Button Cuff

THIS ELEGANT WRIST CUFF requires only the simplest of sewing skills and is a wonderful way to jazz up a plain sweater. It also provides a decorative way to re-use pretty, old-fashioned buttons salvaged from discarded garments. Pearl buttons like these, once used on everyday clothing, are now expensive to buy, but the glass beads mixed in with them make the perfect contrast to the softness of old pearls. Before cutting the ribbon, measure your wrist and adjust the sizing if necessary.

Materials

8in. (20cm) length smoky pink velvet ribbon, 2in. (5cm) wide

White bonded nylon, for sewing on buttons

27 assorted small pearl buttons

10 small flower-shaped pearl buttons

35 faceted ⅛in. (3mm) metallic-coated pink glass beads

6in. (15cm) length rat tail, to match the smoky pink ribbon (rat tail is a satin ribbon woven in the round, looking rather like a rat's tail!)

Gray silk, for lining, 8 x 3in. (20 x 7.5cm)

Matching sewing thread

Needle and pins

Scissors

How to make a Pearl Button Cuff

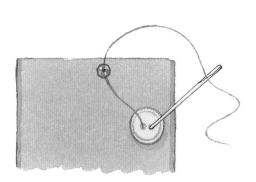

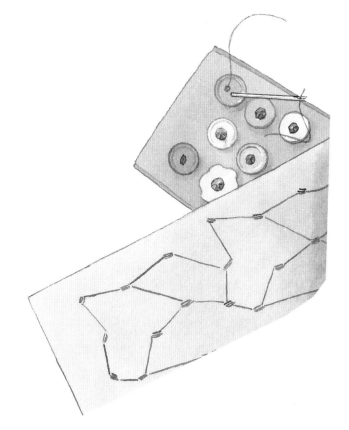

1 (Above) Using the bonded nylon thread, sew on the first button approximately ¾in. (2cm) from the end of the ribbon. Bring the thread through again and sew a glass bead centrally onto the button. Pulling firmly, sew a couple of stitches onto the back of the ribbon to secure the button and bead in place.

2 (Above) Sew on all the beads and buttons in this way, spacing them equally and placing the flower buttons in a random pattern. Sew the last two buttons at the other end of the ribbon ¼in. (6mm) from the end and ¾in. (2cm) apart. Secure them firmly, without adding a top bead as these will be used to fasten the cuff.

TIP: When making your selection of old buttons for the cuff, remember that it is the variety and the unique marks of age in the buttons that make up much of their appeal. Look for sun-bleached buttons, worn textures, and variations of shade as you choose. For an authentic vintage look, work within a single color range, but do not try to match each button too carefully.

3 (Right) Turn the ribbon over onto the wrong side. Turn over each end by ½in. (13mm). Pin in place. Make two loops from the rat tail and tack them in place at one end, behind the first two buttons sewn on.

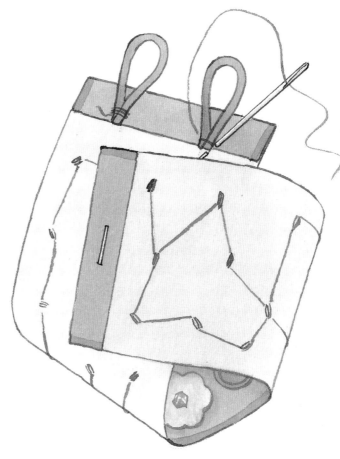

4 Turn a hem on the gray silk with pins. Baste the lining down. Iron it carefully and place it wrong-side down on the ribbon underside.

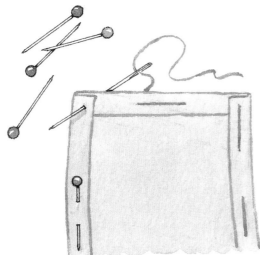

5 (Above) Sew the lining to the ribbon by hand, using small stitches and matching thread. Ensure the loops are secure.

Cut-Glass Pendant Necklace

*T*HIS GLISTENING PENDANT NECKLACE is very theatrical and perfect for eveningwear. Look in flea markets, charity shops, or thrift stores for similar pendants with metal loops on the back. A combination of clear pressed glass beads and bronze seed beads with silver spacers gives an antique appearance. Crystal beads are expensive but they do add the occasional sparkle, so it's good to use them with less expensive pressed glass.

Materials

Large cut-glass theatrical pendant

Silver tiger tail (nylon-coated stainless steel wire)

6 small gold crimp beads

½in. (13mm) spring clasp

½in. (13mm) jump ring

¹⁄₁₆in. (2mm) bronze seed beads

20 ¼in. (6mm) bicone glass crystals

10 ¼in. (6mm) fire-polished faceted glass beads

6 ½in. (13mm) pressed India (pomegranate seed) glass beads

2 ½in. (13mm) fire-polished faceted glass beads

4 ½in. (13mm) pressed glass rondels

28 silver rondel spacers

Wirecutters

Pliers

How to make a Cut-Glass Pendant Necklace

1 (Left) Cut a 28in. (70cm) length of tiger tail and thread the pendant onto the center. Thread a crimp bead onto the tiger tail on each side of the pendant. Crush the beads at the point where they meet the channel on the pendant back.

2 (Right) Start threading the necklace symmetrically, spacing the glass crystal beads with bronze seed beads and silver spacers.

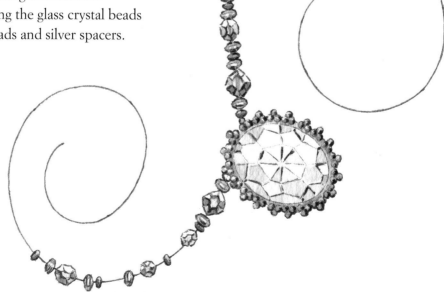

3 (Right) Continue threading the necklace until you reach the required length or you have used all your beads. Before the last two beads, add a crimp bead; crush to hold the beads firmly in place. Thread another crimp bead, followed by a seed bead and a final bicone crystal. Thread the tiger tail through the spring clasp, back through the last two beads and the loose crimp bead. Pull tightly and crush the crimp bead firmly to hold in place. Repeat on the other end with the jump ring to finish.

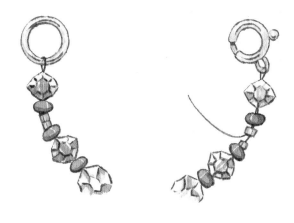

Three-Strand Graded Pearl Necklace

*T*HIS EXTREMELY ELEGANT REAL PEARL NECKLACE has been created from an old necklace which was looking rather the worse for wear. After carefully dismantling the necklace, the damaged pearls were discarded, while the good ones and the pretty jeweled clasp were washed gently. Sort the pearls into sizes before you start. If you do not have an old necklace to re-use, buy a string of graded artificial pearls and a clasp designed to hold three strands.

Materials

Approximately 49 graded real pearls (or freshwater pearls), ⅛—⅜in. (3—9.5mm) in diameter

Silver tiger tail (nylon-coated stainless steel wire)

102 silver ½in. (0.5mm) crimp beads

Pliers

Jeweled clasp for a three-strand necklace

Wirecutters

How to make a Three-Strand Graded Pearl Necklace

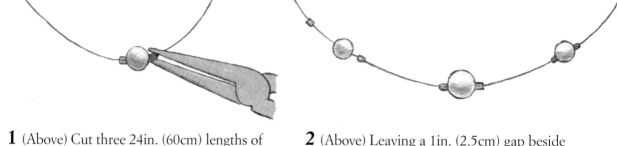

1 (Above) Cut three 24in. (60cm) lengths of tiger tail. Sort your pearls into graded sizes. On the first length of tiger tail, thread a large pearl and place in the center. Thread a crimp bead on both sides of this pearl and crush to hold the pearl in place.

2 (Above) Leaving a 1in. (2.5cm) gap beside the last bead, thread on a crimp bead, squash into place with the pliers, add another pearl, and similarly squash another crimp bead on the other side to hold the pearl in place.

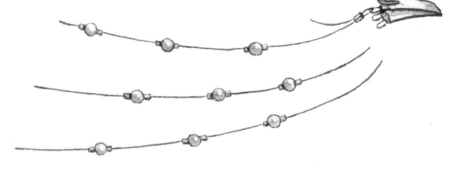

3 (Right) Continue spacing the pearls on the tiger tail in this manner, grading the sizes and slightly reducing the space between the pearls each time until there are eight pearls on each side of the central pearl, making 17 in total. Make sure the sides are symmetrical.

4 (Left) Thread two more lengths of tiger tail in the same way, one with 14 pearls and one with 18. Remember to grade the sizes from large in the center to the smallest at each end. Bring the three ends together, staggering the final small pearls. Thread each end through a crimp bead, then around each ring of the clasp and back through the crimp bead. Squash with pliers to secure. Cut off any excess wire. Repeat on the other side of the clasp.

Three-Strand Turquoise Necklace

ALTERNATIVE

MADE IN EXACTLY THE SAME WAY as the pearl necklace on the previous pages, this turquoise necklace is fastened with a contemporary hook and eye clasp. The veined small turquoise nuggets are randomly spaced and held apart by applying crimp beads on either side of the stones. Silver and blue make a classic color combination that always works well. Although turquoise is classed as a semi-precious stone, it is not very expensive to buy.

Blue-and-White China Cameo Brooches

*T*HESE TRADITIONAL-STYLE CAMEO BROOCHES are an ingenious way of using pieces of antique blue-and-white china as a basis for an elegant piece of jewelry. The finer the china, the nicer the brooch. Cut-glass beads and bronze seed beads provide the perfect finishing touches.

Materials

Broken china (or old, favorite damaged plate or cup) with definable motifs

Tile nippers

⅛in. (3mm) blue cut-glass beads

¹⁄₂₄in. (1mm) and ¹⁄₁₆in. (2mm) bronze seed beads

Thin copper wire

Epoxy glue

Toothpick

Brooch back pins

Wirecutters

Tweezers

How to make Blue-and-White China Cameo Brooches

1 (Left) Identify a motif from your discarded china. Using the tile nippers, cut it out roughly from the larger piece of china. Refine the shape into an oval by gently nipping away at the china until you have the required shape. Leave enough margin around your motif for the bead frame.

2 (Right) Thread the larger bronze seed beads and the blue cut-glass beads alternately onto the wire. You will need to thread enough beads so that the wire is long enough to reach all around the outer rim of the china shard. Twist the two ends of the wire together to create a loop.

3 (Left and below) Mix up some epoxy glue according to the packet instructions and carefully apply it around the rim of the china, using a tooth pick. Quickly push the threaded bead frame into place and hold until the glue has set.

4 (Right) Snip off the excess wire. Mix up some more glue and apply it onto the outer edge of the flat surface of the china, next to the bead rim. Using tweezers, place the smaller seed beads around the edge, making sure they butt up against the glass bead frame. Work quickly but carefully. You may have to work small sections at a time if the glue sets too quickly.

5 (Left) Turn the brooch over and stick the brooch pin centrally onto the back. Allow the glue to set. (If the brooch back is slightly curved, bend the pin to fit snugly into shape.)

Antique Button Flowers

MANY PEOPLE HAVE A BUTTON BOX which has been handed down through generations. This collection will often feature a special antique pearl or ornate metal button which could form the basis of this project. These carefully selected buttons are used to create the center of a rather sumptuous flower, surrounded by petals made by threading tiny beads on to fine wire. A restrained palette of bronze, gold, purple, and lilac has been used. It is important to consider the color if the beads shine and glisten, as too much color can confuse a design. For the best effect choose buttons that are faceted, etched, engraved, or embossed as this will help to reflect the light. These flowers are designed to be worn as a corsage; for a simpler effect pin one singly onto a favorite dress, instantly converting it into an evening outfit. Experiment with using the flowers as shoe buckles or hair ornaments, or to decorate a plain silk evening bag.

Materials

Gold 28-gauge beading wire

Assorted seed beads in brass, gold, lilac, and purple

Selection of antique pearl and metal buttons

Assorted ¼in. (6mm) bugle beads in deep purple, iridescent purple, and dark gold

Wirecutters

How to make Antique Button Flowers

1 (Right) Cut a 24in. (60cm) length of beading wire. Thread one end with 21 brass seed beads, fold over the threaded section of the wire, and twist tightly to form a loop.

2 (Right) Leave a ¼in. (6mm) gap before creating another loop. Continue in this way until you have made seven loops.

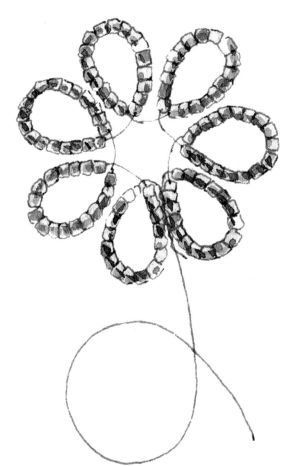

3 (Left) Bring all these loops around to form a neat circle of petals. Twist the two ends of wire together tightly.

4 (Below) On the back of the chosen button, thread the twisted wire-end through the button hole. Wind it around, back and forth, and in and out of the hole and in between the petals to bind it tightly.

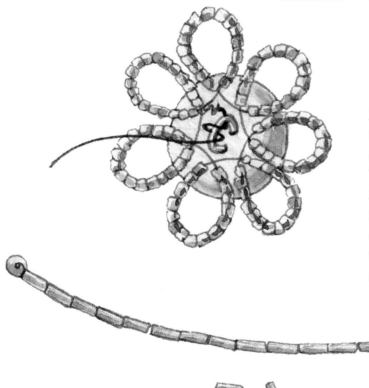

5 (Below) To make a stem, cut a 16in. (40cm) length of wire. Fold it in half and thread a seed bead in the middle. Then bring the two ends through 20 gold bugle beads. Wind the two ends firmly around the back of the flower and in and out of the petals. Finish by winding tightly around the top of the stem, and cut off the excess wire.

Party Pieces

WHO DOESN'T LOVE DRESSING UP—and what better way is there to make an impression than to add an eye-catching piece of jewelry to your outfit. You could be adventurous and don a tiara—the rosebud tiara is ideal for a wedding, and the inclusion of paper rosebuds means it will last forever as a memory of an important day. The pearl and crystal tassel necklace uses pink elongated freshwater pearls interspersed with crystals. The pearls and crystals are expensive to buy, but cost a fraction of a ready-made necklace using the same materials; and you can achieve a similar effect with artifical pearls. A number of projects in this chapter use beads threaded in an interesting design onto multi-strands of beading wire. This is a satisfying technique which extends the creative possibilities of your beading skills; the glass pearl filigree choker and the intricate beaded butterflies show what you can achieve with even simple techniques and are both very rewarding to make.

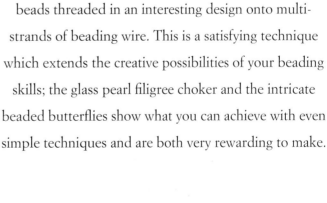

Pink Jeweled Choker

THIS CHOKER is made on four strands of wire which alternately thread through large cut-glass beads, then separate into three strands to thread an oval of seed beads surrounding a single bead on a central wire. The flat-backed pink jewels are recycled from a cheap-and-cheerful elasticated bracelet bought in a flea market. These jewels characteristically have two thread holes on the back. The deep pink jewels partnered with red seed beads make a striking color combination.

Materials

Fine steel wire

2 ⅛in. (3mm) silver crimps

⅝in. (1.5cm) silver lobster claw clasp

12 luster glass beads, ¼in. (6mm) long

7 flat metal-backed acrylic jewels with two thread
   holes, approximately ⅝in. (1.5cm) long

6 pressed glass amethyst color beads

1/16in. (2mm) red and silver-lined rainbow seed beads

Oval jump ring

3in. (7.5cm) length large linked silver chain

Silver eye pin

Pliers

Wirecutters

How to make a Pink Jeweled Choker

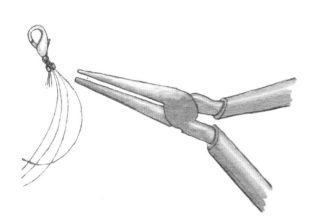

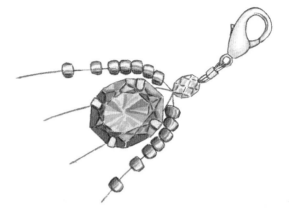

1 (Above) Cut four lengths of wire, each 31½in. (80cm) long. Thread all four through the crimp bead and then through the small ring on the lobster claw clasp. Bend them over and back again through the crimp bead (it may be easier to thread the wires through one at a time). Pull tightly and squash the crimp bead with the pliers. Cut off the excess wire.

2 (Above) Thread all four wires through the first luster glass bead. Open up the wires, threading the two central ones through the two channels on the back of a pink jewel. Take each of the remaining two wires around each side of the jewel and thread each with enough seed beads to surround the jewel (here there are 14 seed beads).

3 (Above) Bring the four wires together again and thread through the second glass bead. Keep the two central wires together, opening out the two outer wires. Create an echo of the oval of the pink jewel by threading 14 seed beads on the outer two wires. On the central two wires, thread four seed beads followed by the amethyst bead. Thread another four seed beads and bring all the wires together to thread through another glass bead.

4 (Above) Continue until you have six jewels and five bead ovals, ending with a pink jewel. Add the final glass bead. Thread the wires through the crimp bead and through the jump ring. Thread the last amethyst bead onto the eye pin. Cut off the extra length of the eye pin, leaving ¼in. (6mm) to thread through the last link of the chain. Bend over the remaining wire and close the loop. Open the jump ring slightly and thread the other end of the chain into it. Close with the pliers.

Pink Jewel Drop Earrings

ALTERNATIVE

*T*HESE DAZZLING DROP EARRINGS have been designed to match the pink jeweled choker on the previous pages and are created from the same beads. A single wire is first threaded through a small, fire-polished cut-glass bead. This is then folded over and the two ends threaded through first a pink jewel and then a luster glass bead. These two wires are threaded through the pink jewel and again through a larger luster glass bead. Unlike the choker, the surrounding circlet of tiny seed beads has been threaded onto a separate wire, which is twisted around the base and then double twisted around the top of the pink jewel to secure it in place. A crimp bead has been used to fix the pretty beaded drop onto the silver fish hook.

Pretty Party Rings

*T*HESE SWEET LITTLE RINGS are so simple and quick to make that you could create several to match your changing mood and outfits. There is such a range of decorative beads available at specialist bead shops that the possibilities of design are endless. Either make a feature of a single bead, as in the case of the silver heart, or create a combination like the circlet of green and turquoise flowers. The simplicity of this design is that the ring part that circles the finger is made from small beads threaded onto fine beading elastic. Crimp beads, when squashed onto the elastic, hold the ring in place and are a much neater way of fixing than tying the two ends together, which often reveals an untidy knot. As these rings are inexpensive to make and so simple in their construction, they are particularly suitable as a starting project for children to try. They would make good stocking stuffers or fun party favors at any time.

Materials

Clear, fine beading elastic

3 green and 3 turquoise sparkly flower beads

¹⁄₁₆in. (2mm) turquoise glass seed beads

3 silver crimp beads

Scissors

Pliers

How to make Pretty Party Rings

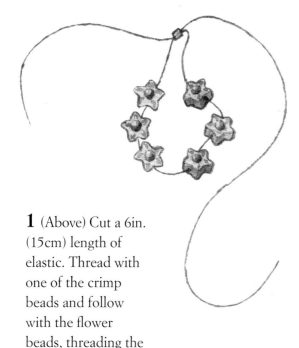

1 (Above) Cut a 6in. (15cm) length of elastic. Thread with one of the crimp beads and follow with the flower beads, threading the colors alternately. Take the other end of the elastic back through the original crimp bead from the other side and pull the elastic slightly to create a circle. Squash the crimp bead with the pliers to secure and cut off any excess elastic.

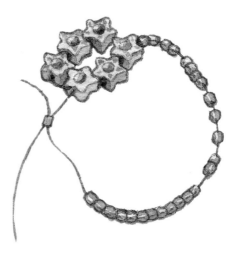

2 (Above) Cut an 8in. (20cm) length of elastic. Thread through the second crimp bead and then through one side of the flower circle, made up of the three flower beads. Thread approximately 25 seed beads onto this elastic and bring it up around and through the second crimp bead, from the other side, as before. Check that the ring fits your finger, adding or removing beads to adjust the size. Squash the crimp bead firmly to create the ring. Cut off any excess elastic.

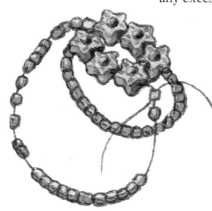

3 (Left) Repeat the same process through the other half of the flower circle to create another adjacent ring fixing it with the third crimp bead.

Beaded Butterflies

*T*HESE EXQUISITE BEADED BUTTERFLIES continue a long tradition of decorative beadwork, using a technique apparent among many different cultures, ranging from tribal to Classical. The enduring shape of the butterfly lends itself to the intricate threading of a variety of beads onto fine metal wire. The wings feature a pattern that is enhanced by the inclusion of jewels in a decorative metal setting with two holes to thread through, thus enabling different methods of construction. The butterflies could be used as a beaded decoration on a pretty, metallic organdy dress, worn as an emblem or brooch, or used as hair barrettes. A good bead shop will also supply metal barrettes with holes through which the butterfly can be attached. Keep to a very simple range of colors, distinguishing each wing by copying nature and using a different color combination. Before creating your design, it may be a good idea to look at butterfly patterns in a book, or try observing the butterflies themselves in summer. You will see how it is possible to mimic the iridescence so common in nature with the use of carefully selected beads.

Materials

Selection of glass seed beads—turquoise, iridescent blue, and clear

Blue and turquoise cut-glass beads (for the ends of the antennae)

Larger cut-glass purple and turquoise beads (for the heads)

Turquoise and deep purple bugle glass beads

Double-holed metal beads with jeweled centers

Small silver crimp beads

½in. (0.5mm) silver beading wire

Wirecutters

Pliers

How to make Beaded Butterflies

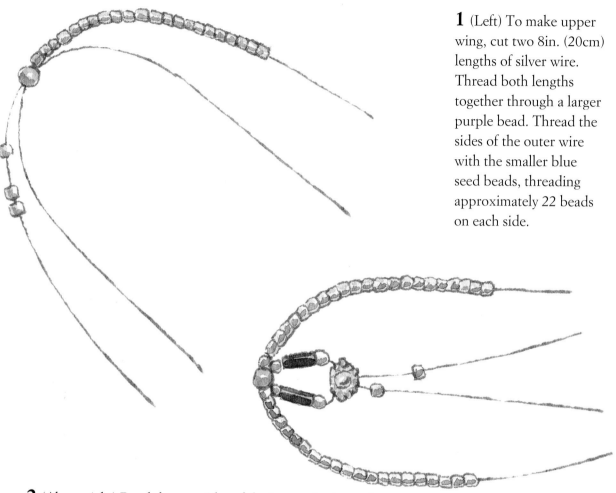

1 (Left) To make upper wing, cut two 8in. (20cm) lengths of silver wire. Thread both lengths together through a larger purple bead. Thread the sides of the outer wire with the smaller blue seed beads, threading approximately 22 beads on each side.

2 (Above right) Bend the two sides of the inner wire inward. Thread each side identically with a small blue seed bead, followed by a purple bugle, another blue seed bead, then thread the two parallel wires together through the double-holed jewel. Repeat the pattern of beading until you have three further sets of bugles.

3 (Right) Thread all four wires through a blue seed bead, two from each side, then pull the wires to tighten the beads. Make another identical wing in the same manner. Make the two smaller wings using fewer green seed beads and bugles.

4 (Left) To make the body, cut two 12in. (30cm) lengths of wire. Thread a larger blue seed bead into the center and fold over to create two ends. Bring them together and thread both through a similar bead, open the wire out, and thread onto each side a purple bugle, followed by a blue seed bead. Thread the two wires through the double-holed jewel, and continue in this way until three jewels are in place.

5 (Left) Thread both wires through a larger purple seed bead and then through a faceted purple glass bead. Open out the wires into antennae and thread with alternate silver and blue seed beads (approximately 13 on each side). Finish the antennae with small blue faceted glass beads, followed by a small silver crimp bead. Press to close and cut off any excess wire.

6 (Left) To assemble the uppermost wings to the body, wind the spare wire around the larger purple seed bead, then twist them together on the back of the body to secure, and cut off the excess wire. Repeat with the smaller wings around the double-holed jewel.

Silver Filigree Necklaces

*T*HESE DELICATE NECKLACES, designed to be worn around a bare neck, look more complicated than they actually are. The sparseness of the beading is accomplished by the use of silver crimp beads. The pretty evenness of the loops is made possible by the use of colored nylon-coated stainless steel wire which has an innate springiness, meaning that the structure of the wire will never lose its shape. Once you have mastered this technique of threading the beads, it is a good idea to make one or two more examples to extend your color range. The use of the iridescent drop beads at the base of the silver loops on the paler necklace is particularly effective, but small seed pearls with a drop pearl edge would work just as well. The same technique can be used to create matching bracelets and earrings.

Materials

NECKLACE 1

60in. (1.5m) pink tiger tail (nylon-coated
    stainless steel wire)

22 ⅛in. (3mm) faceted glass fire-polished pink beads

22 ⅛in. (3mm) faceted glass fire-polished silver
    beads

22 ⅛in. (3mm) faceted glass fire-polished gold beads

⅜in. (9.5mm) spring ring and jump ring silver
    necklace fastener

8 ¹⁄₁₆in. (2mm) silver crimp beads

2 ⅛in. (3mm) silver crimp beads

Wirecutters

Flat-nosed pliers

NECKLACE 2

60in. (1.5m) silver tiger tail (nylon-coated
    stainless steel wire)

19 small glass blue-pink frosted rondels

10 similar teardrop glass beads

10 ½in. (13mm) iridescent glass flat drop beads

2 ⅛in. (3mm) faceted glass pink metalic beads

⅜in. (9.5mm) spring ring and jump ring silver
    necklace fastener

27 ⅛in. (3mm) iridescent glass bugle beads

57 ¹⁄₁₆in. (2mm) silver crimp beads

2 ⅛in. (3mm) silver crimp beads

How to make Silver Filigree Necklaces

1 (Right) To make the first necklace, at one end of the tiger tail, thread in order a pink, silver, gold, and a second silver glass bead. Bring the long end of the tiger tail around counterclockwise to form a loop by threading the end back through the first pink bead. Make sure that you leave at least 6in. (15cm) of tiger tail free at the end.

2 (Right) On the other end of the tiger tail (the long end) thread a pink, a silver, and then a gold bead. Bring the tiger tail around in the same way to create a second loop, this time threading it back through the silver bead on the left side of the first loop. Continue back through the second pink bead, pulling gently to make a matching loop.

3 Thread the next loop in the same way and continue until you have 14 loops. You can adjust the size by pulling gently to make the loops even. It works well to have the loops in the center slightly larger, then tapering toward the ends.

4 (Right) Thread a crimp bead ½in. (13mm) away from the pink bead on the first loop, and press shut firmly with the pliers. Thread five beads in alternate colors, followed by another crimp bead, and press shut again. Leave another ½in. (13mm) space and repeat, creating another identical row of five beads.

5 (Above) Thread a larger crimp bead, followed by a single pink bead. Bring the tiger tail around the jump ring, and back through the bead and crimp ring. Adjust so that all this is ½in. (13mm) away from the last group of beads. Pull the tiger tail gently so the ring sits close to the pink bead, and firmly press the crimp bead shut. Cut off any excess wire with the wirecutters.

Glass Pearl Filigree Choker

ALTHOUGH THIS STUNNING CHOKER looks very intricate, once you have tried and understood the technique it becomes quite easy to make. It is essentially threaded onto three strands of green beading wire which separate and come together, and are threaded in differing ways to create this lovely necklace. When viewed close up, the little pinky-green pearls are shaped like tiny meringues, making a pleasant change to the more regular shape of beads. The tiny, clear glass beads provide an interesting contrast and show the shiny green wire through their centers.

Materials

28-gauge green beading wire

38 ¼in. (6mm) pinky-green glass pearls

6 ⅜in. (9.5mm) pinky-green glass pearls

⅛in. (3mm) clear glass seed beads

⅜in. (9.5mm) split ring

⅝in. (1.5cm) hook fastener

Wirecutters

Pliers

How to make a Glass Pearl Filigree Choker

1 (Above) Cut three 36in. (90cm) lengths of wire. Hold the three ends and twist them twice together 2in. (5cm) from the end, to join them securely. Thread a small glass pearl onto the middle wire, open up the outer wires, and thread six seed beads onto each side.

2 (Above) Bring the outer threaded wires back into and around the glass pearl on the central wire. Twist the three wires together again twice before repeating the same process, but this time threading a larger glass pearl onto the central wire. Thread eight seed beads on the outer wires around the larger pearl, then bring the wires together around the pearl, and twist together again twice.

3 (Right) Thread a small glass pearl on each of the outer wires, twist the wire around ⅜in. (9.5mm) from the last twist, add two more beads in the same manner at ⅜in. (9.5mm) intervals. Thread 12 seed beads onto the central wire.

4 (Left) Bring the wires together and twist as before. Thread a larger glass pearl onto the central wire and, as before, surround it with eight seed beads on each side. Twist again and repeat this pattern until there are six opened out sections and six larger pearls in between. Finish with a matching smaller pearl, as in step 1.

5 (Left) At one end open out the three wires. After ⅜in. (9.5mm), bend one of the wires over the split ring, return, and cut off at ⅜in. (9.5mm) or just before the first beads are threaded. Cut the second wire at ¼in. (6mm). Finally, bind the third wire neatly and tightly around the ⅜in. (9.5mm) between the first beads and the split ring. Cut off the excess wire. Repeat at the other end of the choker, attaching the hook fastener.

Filigree Glass Bead Bracelet

ALTERNATIVE

MADE IN EXACTLY THE SAME WAY as the choker on the previous pages, this filigree bracelet is so much more delicate as it is made on finer wire with smaller beads. Beading wire comes in two thicknesses (the finer gauge is used here) and in many colors, meaning that the actual wire structure of your piece of jewelry can become a prominent and decorative part of your design. Choose your beads and wire colors together. The little, round, lustrous lilac beads are held in place by twisting the wire around the outside of each bead. Smoky pink beads are also used; unlike the seed beads, these have straight sides and so sit evenly together.

Ribbon Rosette

THIS STRIKING VARIATION ON THE THEME OF BEADED JEWELRY is created by combining a bold spotted ribbon with a vintage button and silver beads. The button used as a centerpiece is surrounded by "rays" of teardrop silver beads and the rosette is made by simply folding and cross-looping the ribbon into six "petals." Although the restrained black-and-white color palette has been used to match a simple, smart everyday outfit, the same technique may be used in a much more flamboyant and colorful way, perhaps using more precious and jewel-like antique beads. A smaller rosette would look wonderful as a central motif on a velvet choker or a head band.

Materials

Pins

24in. (60cm) woven black satin
   ribbon with white spots, ½in.
   (13mm) wide

24in. (60cm) plain black ribbon for
   lining, ½in. (13mm) wide

Strong black thread and needle

6 ½in. (13mm) silver teardrop beads

6 ⅛in. (3mm) silver seed beads

1 vintage button with silver ray
   design or one from your collection

1in. (2.5cm) circular brooch back

Epoxy glue

Scissors

How to make a Ribbon Rosette

1 Pin together the two ribbons, the plain black covering the underside of the spotted ribbon. Stitch the ribbons together close to each edge.

2 (Above) Cut the ribbon into three lengths, each of 8in. (20cm). Find the center point of each length of ribbon and mark with a pin. For each ribbon length, twist one end (spotty ribbon facing you) around, bringing it back to overlap the middle point by ½in. (13mm).

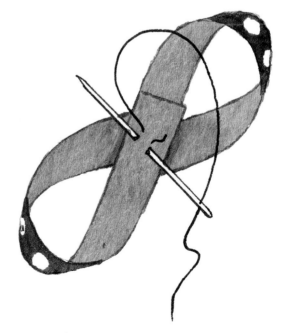

3 (Right) Turn the loop around (black ribbon lining facing you) and repeat with the other end of the ribbon, overlapping and securing in the same way to create a figure-of-eight.

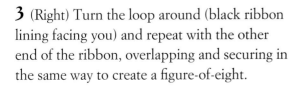

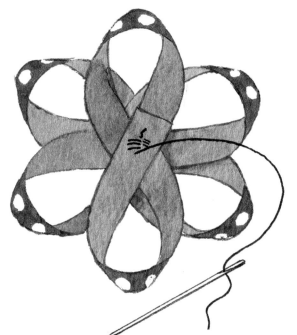

4 (Left) Place the three figure-of-eights on top of one another, center on center, so that they form a six-petal rosette. Stitch through all layers to secure in place.

5 (Right) Spotty side up, sew the six teardrop beads topped with the seed beads equidistantly around the center, to form an innter "flower." Sew the vintage button into the center of the rosette. Turn the rosette over and stick the brooch back on with the epoxy glue. Allow the glue to dry.

Grosgrain Ribbon
with Bow

ALTERNATIVE

*T*HE LOVELY DUSKY PINK OF ANTIQUE GROSGRAIN RIBBONS combined with pretty, sparkling crystals gives this bead-and-ribbon project an authentic vintage feel, enhanced by the use of a 1940s plastic belt buckle. Iridescent bicone crystals have been fitted into the grooves of the buckle and a stunning faceted droplet hangs beneath between the tails of the bow. Use a striking combination of styles and materials, delicate and bold, natural and man-made, dull and sparkly, and the result will be an adornment that cannot fail to be noticed. The ribbon used here has been lined with a finer satin ribbon, which is subtly revealed on the hems on the tails of the bow.

Memory Wire Bracelet

*T*HIS SIMPLE PROJECT can be made from assorted leftover beads. Steel memory wire keeps its shape and can be used without any need to attach clasps, making it ideal for this stylish bracelet. Finish the wire-ends with larger beads to make a bold, decorative statement. And why not make a set of matching necklace and earrings with similar beads, or a selection of Indian-style bracelets, and wear several together for even greater impact?

Materials

Bracelet length of memory wire
5 foil-lined glass beads with rosebud design
Assorted short bugle beads in silver, gold, and metallic pink

Assorted small, faceted, fire-polished glass beads in pastel colors
2 large teardrop foil-lined glass beads
Pliers

How to make a Memory Wire Bracelet

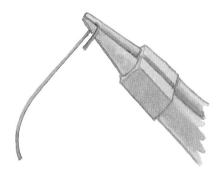

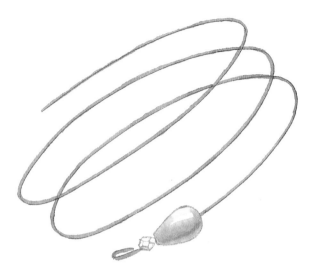

1 (Above) Using the pliers, turn one end of the memory wire back on itself to form a small, neat loop. This will prevent the beads sliding off the wire.

2 (Above) Thread a small faceted glass bead onto the wire, followed by a large teardrop bead (small end first) and push them right up to the looped end of the wire.

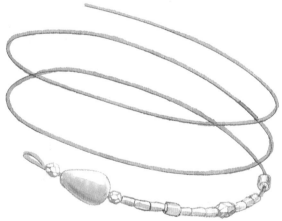

3 (Above) Now thread all remaining beads onto the wire, except the remaining teardrop bead and a small faceted glass bead. Place the beads randomly, spacing out the faceted glass beads and the rosebud beads with the assorted pink, gold, and silver bugle beads. Try to achieve a pleasing sequence of colors and shapes.

4 (Above) When all the beads have been threaded on, finish off with another teardrop bead (this time, push the bulbous end on first) and a small faceted glass bead. Twist the wire end over into a tightly closed loop, using the pliers.

Pale Crystal Looped Earrings

*T*HESE DELICATE, ELEGANT EARRINGS are created using pale, faceted, fire-polished glass beads, bicone crystals, and tiny silver bugles. They are all threaded onto a loop made from tiger tail. Fastened at the top with two crimp beads, the loop of the gold fish hook earrings fits between these two beads. A larger fire-polished, metallic-finish faceted bead has been threaded onto the base of the fish hook and a single foil-lined rosebud glass bead defines the base of the loop.

Cluster Earrings

*T*HESE STRIKING EARRINGS would look wonderfully glamorous with an evening dress, yet they are very easy to make. Some bead shops sell bags of mixed beads in different colors and sizes which would be suitable for this design, or you could use up beads left over from other jewelry projects. These faceted, iridescent glass beads and bronze seed beads are first woven onto a sieve. After the beads are attached, snap the earring backs firmly into place, thus neatly covering all the working wires. Work out a good mix of colors and finishes before you start by putting a collection of beads together, choosing subtle contrasts of shape and different hues and tones.

Materials

2 earring backs with sieves, 1¼in. (3cm) in diameter

⅛in. (3mm) or 34-gauge copper beading wire

Assorted faceted glass beads—some iridescent, some
   teardrop, some long—in turquoise, green, and blue

¹⁄₁₆in. (2mm) bronze seed beads

Wirecutters

How to make Cluster Earrings

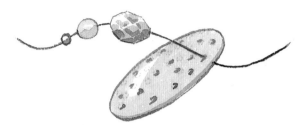

1 (Above) Cut a workable length of wire, say 24in. (60cm). From behind, thread through an outer hole on the sieve, leaving a tail of 2in. (5cm) on the back. On the convex side, add an elongated iridescent bead, followed by a smaller clear glass bead, then thread on a bronze seed bead.

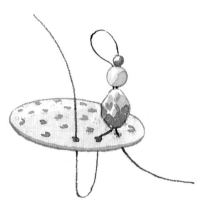

2 (Right) Bring the wire back down through the two faceted beads and through an adjacent hole. Pull tightly to anchor the beads firmly, then push the wire up through the next hole.

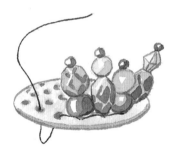

3 (Above) Add another group of three beads adjacent to the first group, varying the colors and shapes of the beads slightly to provide a subtle contrast. Continue adding selections of beads three at a time, topped by a bronze seed bead. Remember to pull tightly each time you thread the wire through the back of the sieve to hold the beads securely.

4 (Above) When you have added sufficient beads to make a tight cluster, pull the wire through to the back. Twist the ends together to secure, and cut off any excess wire. Place the sieve on top of the earring back and clip the tabs over to hold it securely in place. Create a matching earring in the same manner.

Rosebud Wedding Tiara

*T*HIS CHARMING TIARA is made from a delicate combination of acrylic beads, glass stamens, and tiny, white paper rosebuds. It would be perfect for a bride or bridesmaid, or for a summer garden party. It's a lovely present to make and the colors can be chosen to suit different occasions, such as white or cream for a bride, or to match a bridesmaid's dress or a party frock. The flowers are available from a good haberdashery or notions store.

Materials

34-gauge fine silver beading wire

12 ⅜in. (9.5mm) and 24 ¼in. (6mm) assorted faceted acrylic beads in pale, clear blues and greens

36 ⅛in. (3mm) green seed beads

Slim metal hair band, approximately 14in. (35cm) long

7 paper rosebuds

8 glass bobble stamens

Lime green embroidery thread

White craft glue

Wirecutters

How to make a Rosebud Wedding Tiara

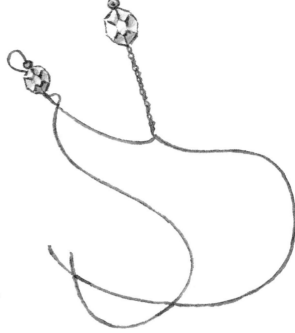

1 (Above) To make the bead buds and flowers, cut 12 lengths of beading wire, each 12in. (30cm) long. Thread one of the green seed beads centrally onto each wire, fold over the wire, and thread the two ends through one of the larger acrylic beads. Twist the wire together tightly to make a ¾in. (2cm) stem.

2 (Above) Bend one of the remaining ends of the wire 1¼in. (3cm) from the twist. Add a smaller acrylic bead followed by a seed bead. Fold over and thread the wire back through the acrylic bead and twist, as before, into a ¾in. (2cm) stem.

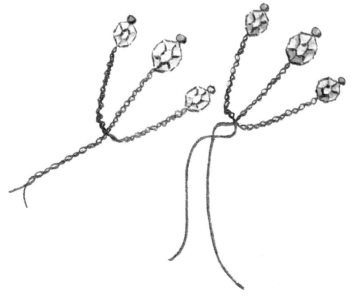

3 (Left) Repeat on the other side, making a sprig of three. Twist the remaining wires together to create a stem. Make 12 identical sprigs in this way.

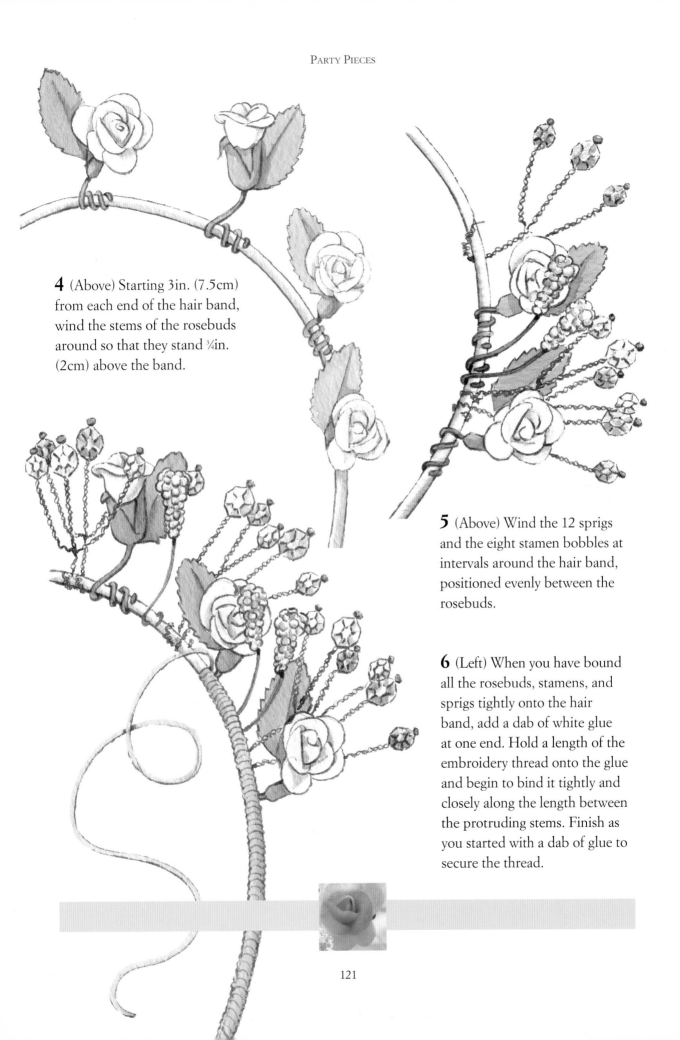

4 (Above) Starting 3in. (7.5cm) from each end of the hair band, wind the stems of the rosebuds around so that they stand ¾in. (2cm) above the band.

5 (Above) Wind the 12 sprigs and the eight stamen bobbles at intervals around the hair band, positioned evenly between the rosebuds.

6 (Left) When you have bound all the rosebuds, stamens, and sprigs tightly onto the hair band, add a dab of white glue at one end. Hold a length of the embroidery thread onto the glue and begin to bind it tightly and closely along the length between the protruding stems. Finish as you started with a dab of glue to secure the thread.

Beaded Flower and Gold Leaf Tiara

ALTERNATIVE

*T*HIS BRIGHTLY COLORED VARIATION of the wedding tiara is very simple to make, but perhaps more suitable for a child. The flowers are made by making open "petals" of seed beads threaded onto short lengths of wire, folded over, and twisted together to form a flower. A contrasting, faceted turquoise glass bead has been added as a center when twisting the flower onto the metal hair band before binding it with a matching turquoise embroidery thread. The pretty stamped-out gold leaves were bought in bunches from a craft shop. A double string of tiny seed beads has also been bound onto the hair band with fine wire.

Pearl and Crystal Tassel Necklace

H ERE, UNUSUAL FRESHWATER PEARLS are interspaced with small oval pearls and rose-colored crystals. These are more expensive materials than used for some of the other projects in this book, but they create a beautiful necklace—a lasting gift with timeless, natural beauty. However, you can make the piece using less costly materials, too. A simple tassel made from complementary beads adds an unusual decorative touch.

Materials

20in. (50cm) pink tiger tail (nylon-coated stainless steel wire)

3 silver crimp beads

⅜in. (9.5mm) spring clasp

26 rose faceted crystals

17 pink ½in. (13mm) long freshwater or artificial pearls

26 pink oval freshwater or artificial pearls

Jump ring

24in. (60cm) fine silver tiger tail

Pliers

Wirecutters

How to make a Pearl and Crystal Tassel Necklace

2 (Left) Thread a crystal onto the tiger tail to butt up against the crimp bead, followed by a small pearl and a longer one. Continue in this way, adding a small pearl either side of the longer one with a crystal in between.

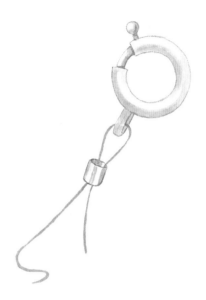

1 (Above) Cut a 20in. (50cm) length of pink tiger tail. Thread one end through a crimp bead, then through the ring on the spring clasp, back through the crimp bead, making sure that the crimp bead is as close to the ring as possible. Crush the crimp bead with pliers to secure. Trim off any excess wire.

3 (Above) After the seventh long pearl, add another long pearl without either smaller ones or crystals between them. This point is where the central tassels will be attached in step 5. Continue threading the crystals and pearls so the pattern matches the first half of the necklace.
When the last crystal is in place, add a crimp bead and again thread the tiger tail through the jump ring, over and back through the crimp bead. Crush the bead lightly with the pliers and pull together. As you squeeze, remember to leave a small gap between the seventh and eighth pearls.

4 (Left) Cut three 8in. (20cm) lengths of the finer tiger tail. Thread a crystal into the middle of each length, fold over, and bring the two ends back through a long pearl. Thread each tassel with four small pearls and three crystals.

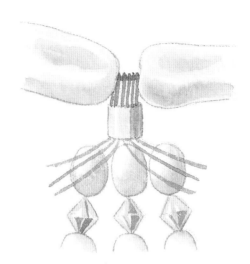

5 (Above) Put the three tassels together and thread all six threads through a crimp bead, pushing this up against the small pearls. Bend the six threads around the tiger tail between the two central long beads. Thread back through the crimp bead once more. Pull each thread so it is evenly pulled through and crush the crimp bead with the pliers. Cut off the excess wire.

Index